Small BUILDINGS

Mike Cadwell

PAMPHLET ARCHITECTURE 17

Princeton Architectural Press

Published by
Princeton Architectural Press
37 East 7th Street
New York, New York 10003
(212) 995-9620

For a free catalog of books, call
(800) 722-6657

Design: Allison Saltzman
Copy editing: Clare Jacobson and Jonathan Bell
Special thanks to: Caroline Green, Therese Kelly,
Bill Monaghan, and Ann C. Urban
—Kevin C. Lippert, publisher

Library of Congress Cataloging-in-Publication Data
Cadwell, Mike, 1952–
Small buildings / Mike Cadwell.
p. cm.
— (Pamphlet architecture ; 17)
ISBN 1-56898-055-8
1. Cadwell, Mike, 1952– —Themes, motives.
2. Outbuildings—United States.
3. Architecture—Research.
I. Title. II. Series:
Pamphlet architecture ; no. 17.
NA737.C23A4 1995
720'.92—dc20   95-24531
CIP

Contents

PREFACE
Mike Cadwell

so much depends
upon
a red wheel
barrow
glazed with rain
water
beside the white
chickens
William Carlos Williams

I would like to thank Princeton Architectural Press for publishing work that has been, until now, private and inaccessible. I am especially pleased to be included in the Pamphlet Architecture series, not only because the size of the pamphlets (small) seems appropriate to these projects (which are also small) but also because the price of the pamphlets is within a student's budget. I think of this work as a beginning and I hope that its publication offers others a way of beginning.

The projects illustrated in the following pages were built by myself. The reason I chose to work this way is simple: the abstractions of modeling, drawing, and writing about architecture became meaningless to me when I no longer knew to what these abstractions referred. It was as if I were a painter composing a painting without a true sense of what it felt like to put pigment to canvas.

But how to seek this sensual knowledge? After an extensive intellectual education, how was I to embark on a sensual education? The inescapable answer was to build. I could not build large because I had no commissions. I did not wish to build for others as a carpenter, mason,

glazier, or steelworker. However, by building small and by using materials simply, I could make a start. The hand and the eye could gain a sense of materials—heft, strength, texture, luminosity.

The central offering of *Small Buildings* is the documentation of one such sensual education. I have worked primarily with wood on rural sites but other materials and other sites are certainly possible and would yield results no less valid. This education has not been prohibitively expensive or technically demanding, nor is it bound by the constraints of clients, codes, and contractors.

A cautionary note. As you read this text and look at the pictures, it is important to remember that words and images are not the essence of this work, or of any work of architecture. Architecture is material giving form to space in light and it can be fully appreciated only by the engagement of the human body. Many of the small buildings still stand and you are welcome to visit them. Better still, build your own.

The only operative principle is to approach building respectfully so that the things of architecture supercede ideas about architecture. I have found that the work takes on its own momentum and one need only be quiet and pay attention. It is mysterious and liberating.

I am grateful to the Graham Foundation for its generous financial support, Charles T. Erickson for his excellent photographs, and many others for their construction assistance, especially Dick Brown, Jason Cadwell, and Jane Murphy.

This book is dedicated to my parents, John Burditt Cadwell and Mary Elizabeth Allen Cadwell.

SMALL BUILDINGS

The tasks which face the human apparatus of perception at the turning points of history cannot be solved by optical means, that is by contemplation, alone. They are mastered gradually by habit, under the guidance of tactile appropriation.
Walter Benjamin

Building
Building is a good solid word. Not just a noun; an object spied in a distant field or an image perused in a magazine. Building is also a verb; a creative act with its own unpredictable unfolding in the physical world. Building as such is not finally determined by the machinations of language or the preconceptions of the studio but demands its own solid ground, its own insightful embrace.

It is the verb "building" that inspires the projects documented here. The projects are built by myself so that I might be immersed in the physicality of architecture. To experience architectural effects more powerfully, the palette is restricted to elemental forms, simple tectonics, basic human acts, and fundamental site relationships.

The strategy of building is not intended as a nostalgic refusal of the broader social obligations of architecture but rather as a beginning, a grounding of architectural understandings in the built environment before applying them to more complex venues. While it is both infeasible and undesirable to maintain a hands-on approach to the increasingly complex construction industry, it is also misguided to generate architecture from a series of hermetic abstractions initiated at a safe remove from concrete reality.

Pastoral Quartet

The first four small buildings were developed as a pastoral quartet. "Pastoral," writes M. H. Abrams in his *Glossary of Literary Terms* (New York: Holt Rinehart & Winston, 1971), "refers to any work which envisions a withdrawal from ordinary life to a place apart, close to the elemental rhythms of nature, where a man achieves a new perspective on life in the real and complex world." Two qualifiers should be added here.

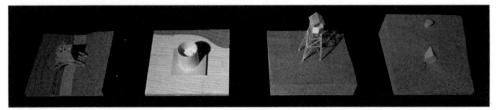

Pastoral Quartet: Bridge-Box, Drum-Barge, Ark-Tower, and House-Tunnel

First, "the elemental rhythms of nature" are not always benevolent. The landscape of New England continually veers towards entropy. This tendency is all the more poignant today with the disintegration of the agrarian order of proud Greek Revival farmsteads presiding over carefully nurtured fields; the houses are now abandoned and the fields lie fallow as a tangle of brush approaches.

Second, while the pastoral experience is intensely private, its overriding purpose is adamantly public. One's meditations in seclusion inevitably affect one's engagement with society at large. While there is a retreat, there is also a return.

Architecturally, the small buildings find their sources in American building archetypes, constructions that address elementary programs with simple forms, basic site relationships, and clear tectonics. Each small building is concerned with a specific pair of forms, a specific pair of activities, and a specific relationship to the earth. As a group, the buildings are unified by their wood construction, their rural setting, and an overall seasonal theme. An outline of these intentions is as follows:

spring	*Bridge-Box*	*walk-sit*	*over water*
summer	*Drum-Barge*	*swim-stand*	*in water*
autumn	*Ark-Tower*	*climb-sit*	*over ground*
winter	*House-Tunnel*	*descend-lie*	*in ground*

The buildings are located on various secluded New England sites and are open to all who find them. The wood is left untreated and will eventually decay, the buildings slowly folding back into the earth.

Airplane hangar, Iowa; Kiva, New Mexico; Coal conveyer, Arizona.

BRIDGE-BOX
Salisbury, Connecticut
1983

Bridge-Box spans a small stream and is entered from either side. The box is nine feet long by six feet wide and contains a ladder-back chair and two rooftop banquettes from which a waterfall is revealed.

Originally, the bridge and the box were mated to produce a decidedly unfortunate hybrid (imagine a covered bridge swallowed by an ice cream truck). At the suggestion of a friend, Michael Hassig, the unhappy pair were pried apart, considered as discrete structures, and allowed to play off one another. The project was enriched when an obsession with design was replaced by an attention to the realities of construction.

Thus, the bridge is a simple truss whose asymmetrical disposition defers to the stream banks' unequal slopes. Likewise, the box is an independent, tightly wrapped volume, a kind of camera whose film is the human observer. The bridge then lifts the box, delicately balancing it above the water and lending a curious weightlessness to the interior space—a space that is intently compressed at the viewing seat and released skyward at the banquettes. At a smaller scale, a similar synergism of form occurs as the ladder-back chair fulfills the promise of its name by facilitating both climbing and sitting.

The materials of Bridge-Box respond to human touch by becoming more refined as the building turns in on itself: from the rough bolted lumber of the bridge, to the finished tongue and groove boards wrapping the box, to the continuous plywood sheathing of the interior.

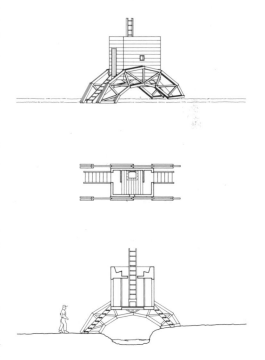

Bridge-Box was built for an exhibition sponsored by *Perspecta 21, The Yale Architectural Journal.*

DRUM-BARGE
Starksboro, Vermont
1985

Drum-Barge floats freely on a secluded pond. Its seven-foot-diameter drum has a pyramidal canvas roof and is supported by four pontoons.

While one hovers above recently thawed spring water in Bridge-Box, one must take a summer plunge to reach Drum-Barge. One swims beneath the drum into the dappled light of the octagonal grotto, hoists oneself up the rope dangling from the roof, pops through the trap door into the body of the drum, and finally stands in sunlight to quietly drift amidst the revolving landscape. Centric buildings are often compromised by entries that privilege a particular side (the Pantheon is a prime example). Here entry is resolved by an ascension through the center, an *axis mundi*, if you will, linking water and sky.

The lineage of the Drum-Barge extends to the water reservoirs of Appalachian railways and to the freight barges of the Mississippi River. The drum, however, is now literally emptied of its original function—it is placed on the water rather than acting as a vessel for water. Its ribbed structure provides a human scale to the interior while its tiny windows boost its exterior scale, giving it a grand presence on the pond. The barge also acquires a skeletal configuration by being broken into smaller sections and laced together with overlapping timbers.

In spite of its rather strict choreography, the Drum-Barge accommodated the varied activities of a broad public: the intimacies of a pair of honeymooners, the siege from small boats piloted by neighborhood children, and the leaping antics of an entire high school track team.

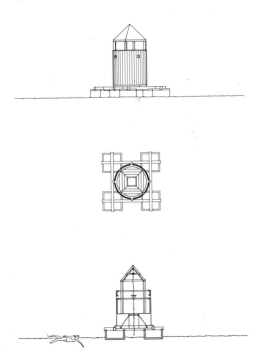

ARK-TOWER
Lakeville, Connecticut
1984

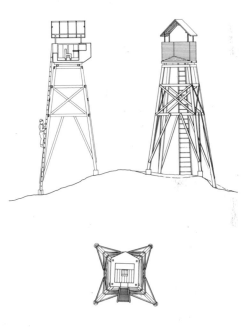

While Bridge-Box and Drum-Barge deal with fundamental site relationships of being above and in water, Ark-Tower and House-Tunnel concentrate on fundamental site relationships of being above and in land.

Ark-Tower stands twenty-five feet tall, a solitary figure stepping up a hillside on the outskirts of a farm. One ascends the tower by a ladder whose telescoping configuration exaggerates one's perception of the climb. Entering the ark, one is reassured by short thick walls that provide a welcome barrier to the precipitous drop while affording a full view of the countryside.

As in previous buildings, there is a kind of democracy of form where each element is allowed its voice in conversation with its equally independent neighbor. The ark has left the water and now floats through the air on canvas wings. It is a vehicle for the imagination, outfitted with cabinets, a foldaway desk, and a rolling chair. The tower strides below, its tapered frame anchored to concrete piers. Accented by its subtle rotation, the ark enters into a tentative agreement with the tower, appearing to nest momentarily.

Particular wood species elaborate upon the sensual effects of the earlier Bridge-Box (where wood details were refined as the building turned inward). The tower's hemlock legs check and fade to a dull gray like old bones, the ark's pine skin, a soft pink at conception, tans to a hard golden brown, and the roof's tightly grained ash frame provides a taut winged armature for the fluttering canvas plumage.

As in all the small buildings, Ark-Tower's wood is left untreated. The pastoral movement from city to country is temporal so the materials of the small buildings celebrate, rather than repress, their fleeting quality.

HOUSE-TUNNEL
Pittsford, Vermont
1986–87

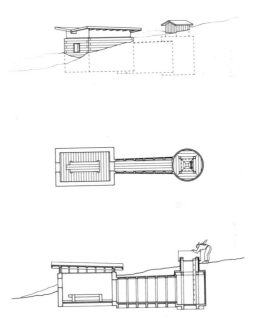

House-Tunnel brings the pastoral quartet of small buildings to a close. It lies buried beneath a pasture's gentle slope as if hibernating—of its thirty-foot length, only the hatchway and part of the house are exposed.

As Drum-Barge is generated by a vertical path leading one out of the water, House-Tunnel is generated by a horizontal path leading one out of the earth. Particular stations on the path are exaggerations of simple American vernacular types: a hatchway of the Midwest is steepened, a kiva from the southwest is compressed, a mining tunnel from the Rocky Mountains is tapered, and a root cellar from New England is finished for human habitation.

The movement out of the earth is keyed by the section of the house. Anchored by a thick subterranean wall of rough timbers on the exterior and smooth plywood on the interior, the house reveals itself as a wainscoted stud frame at ground level, and completes itself at the roof as a spinal skeleton with light metal panels.

The orientation of the House-Tunnel continues the theme of building as a device for locating oneself within the larger landscape. The ability of a building to establish permanent relationships to topography (the slope), landmarks (a distant farm), and climate (the metaphor of hibernation), is expanded to include planetary movements—the axis of House-Tunnel is oriented to the winter solstice.

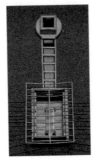

In spite of the rather somber chthonic implication of House-Tunnel, children gleefully run the length of the tunnel, leap onto the bed, and catapult through the window into the snow beyond.

LATER WORK

S ubsequent to the quartet, a set of furniture was fabricated: chairs, a table, a bed, and an armoire. In addition, four more buildings evolved individually as commissions for sculpture parks. Rolling Tower was built at ArtPark, Gatehouse at Socrates Sculpture Park, Rain Drop at the DeCordova Museum, and Observatory is proposed for a private estate. Observations made while building the quartet were developed in the later projects:

Material

Material decisions are not merely the scientific analyses of particular properties but are more often an intuitive, synthetic process driven by bodily experience. Sensual knowledge—

knowledge based upon touch, smell, sight, and sound—is accrued and drawn upon when one is immersed in the process of construction. The complexity of current tectonic systems does not absolve one of the responsibility of intimately understanding them. In fact, a new era of craft may be possible as computers forge a direct link between design and fabrication.

Form

Simple forms and their corresponding spaces possess a remarkable energy. This energy is increased when the forms are juxtaposed (a bridge and a box, for example) or displaced in site or use (as in Observatory, where a cart is hoisted aloft, glides about, and becomes a compass to the heavens). Simple forms are linked to building archetypes and, indeed, have a kinship with the collective archetypes of Jungian psychology. It is also true that juxtaposition and displacement are standard terms in Freudian dream analysis. However, the power of simple forms cannot be reduced to psychological categories or any other single theoretical construct—such forms are strongly multivalent, capable of accommodating a wide range of conscious activities while simultaneously evoking myriad unconscious associations. Finally, the sensual appreciation of form and space is primary and is not bound by language.

Program

Program is a relative condition. In spite of the buildings' rather strict choreographies, they continually subverted their author's more dictatorial aspirations. Betrayals were numerous. Particularly memorable was the siege of the Drum-Barge by an armada of young neighborhood pirates. Simple forms are generously accommodating, insisting only upon moments of activity and repose, the precise natures of which are in a continual state of flux.

Site

Site is a more absolute condition. The history of even the most mundane building will include a variety of conflicting uses but it will inevitably be limited to only one location. While program is subject to the energetic interpretation of individuals, a site locks a building into permanent relationships to local topography, distant landmarks, larger climactic conditions, and astronomical movements. Ideally, architecture becomes a kind of cipher, revealing a site's most profound potentials.

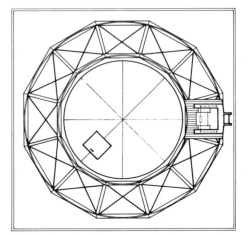

opposite page:
Rolling Tower, construction; Gatehouse, juxtaposition of simple forms; meeting house and machinery shop, Vermont.

this page:
Rain Drop, energetic interpretation of individuals; Observatory, building as cipher.

FURNITURE
Chairs, Table, Bed, Armoire
1985–94

Chairs, 1985 (string of eight): 16' l
Table, 1987: 28" h x 24" w x 48" l
Bed, 1994: 24" h x 54" w x 88" l
Armoire, 1988–91: 84" h x 30" w x 30" d

A set of furniture evolved with the small buildings and share a playful fascination with wood tectonics, simple forms, and mobility. The smoothly planed hardwoods of conventional furniture are here replaced by robust sections of rough pine timbers which are threaded together with steel rods and mounted on standard warehouse casters. On moving day, the furniture can be disassembled and thrown into the back of a truck or, preferably, left intact and towed to a new location.

Chairs are the progeny of Ark-Tower's central perch. It seemed that a herd of these rolling characters would make a jolly grouping and, indeed, carried away by their own good humor, Chairs bolted from their showing at the Yale Art and Architecture Gallery. A pair of Chairs eloped to a more remote location where the Table obliged their restlessness with casters of its own. Presumably, the couple later retired to the Bed, rolled into the night, and took flight under a winged canopy.

On a more somber note, Armoire alludes to its Latin root, *arma*, meaning tools, especially weapons. A lonely and ominous cyclops, Armoire invades the presumed safety of the domestic landscape. Armoire's intentions are not revealed, its contents hidden behind a locked door.

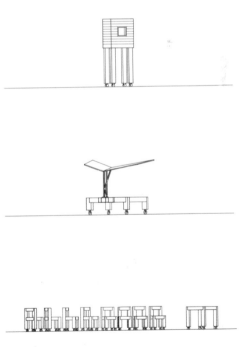

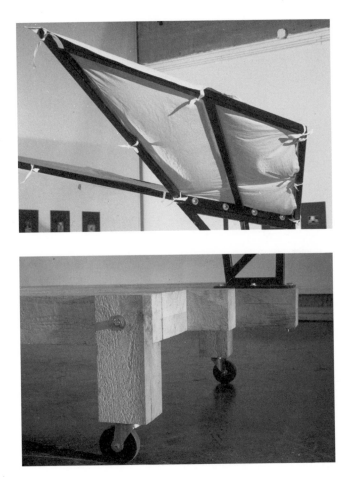

ROLLING TOWER

ArtPark
Lewiston, New York
1986

Rolling Tower stands fourteen feet tall and hoists a viewing box aloft. One mysterious eye and a continuous plywood lining reinforce the box's privacy. Its spatial compression is relieved only by a pair of ear-like skylights.

Rolling Tower's public front is fortified by a dense layer of spruce tongue-and-groove siding and an imposing skeleton of unplaned pine timbers. The tower sports two sets of wheels: oversized warehouse casters to the front and a leaf-spring trailer assembly to the rear.

Through a series of fortuitous misunderstandings, Rolling Tower was never granted a permanent site. While the buildings of the pastoral quartet are locked into particular site relationships, Rolling Tower is a vagabond. The protective seclusion of the box is continually confronted with a variety of public locations.

Paradoxically, Rolling Tower's itinerant nature did not make it any less site specific. Instead, it became a kind of cipher: a sentry standing guard over a sea of parked cars, a stranger poised at the park's wooded boundary, a monument nodding sympathetically to a distant obelisk, a figural statue addressing the entry axis of the park's theater, and a startled traveller stumbling upon an enormous electric generating station. Rolling Tower's chameleon-like character led to an understanding of the primacy of site over program: what a building does is determined by where it is.

GATEHOUSE

Socrates Scultpure Park
Long Island City, New York
1988

Gatehouse crouches at the edge of New York City's East River and eagerly looks to Manhattan. Its viewing box sprouts a set of stout legs, wags a stair at its tail, holds a monumental chair within its belly, and extends a cantilevered bridge at its nose. Gatehouse is six feet wide by thirteen feet tall by twenty-four feet long.

Gatehouse uses many strategies of previous small buildings. Simple forms are juxtaposed: stair against box and box against bridge. These forms, in turn, are displaced: the box is lifted and the bridge is suspended. Basic human acts are framed: climbing, sitting, walking, and standing. Elemental siting relationships are established: above ground and above water. Space is gathered and released in an accordion-like sequence of stair, box, and bridge. And, finally, wood details are refined from the rough 12 by 12 timber of the legs to the smooth plywood lining of the interior.

It is important to note, however, that the celebration of the natural landscape so essential to the quartet is here replaced by the celebration of human engagement in the city. Although the Gatehouse overlooks the East River, this section of the river is not known for its pristine beauty—it is primarily remarkable for its foreboding reputation in Yankee shipping lore as Hell's Gate. Furthermore, and in direct contrast to the framing of a waterfall in the Bridge-Box, the viewing box of the Gatehouse commemorates an otherwise anonymous Manhattan

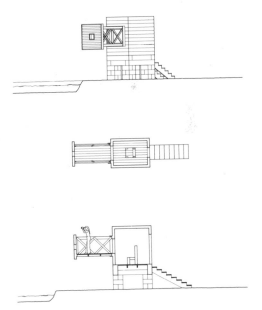

highrise that houses health services. It was hoped that the Gatehouse would act as both guardian of treacherous waters and condenser of a city's history and potential.

RAIN DROP

DeCordova Museum and Sculpture Park
Lincoln, Massachusetts
1992–94

Rain Drop's four timber chairs support the steel structure of a fourteen-foot-square petal roof. The roof gathers rainwater, directs it to a central drain, and drops its onto native rocks embedded in the floor below.

Rain Drop returns to the pastoral theme of the quartet. One leaves one's responsibilities in the city of Boston, travels to the bucolic park of the DeCordova, and rests in a chair to await the fall of rain. The restorative power of the pastoral retreat is reinforced by the numerous revitalizing associations of water.

Intersecting the horizontal movement from city to country, the materials of Rain Drop address the vertical movement from earth to sky. Buried in the earth as concrete, the structure changes to wood at the level of habitation, reaches to the sky with light sections of steel, and catches light and water with thin sheets of translucent fiberglass.

Anchoring these two movements, the siting of Rain Drop roots itself in local topography and global mapping systems as well as registering the larger climate. The chairs gently step down the hillside while their hind legs are planted to true north. The floor provides a level plane for human activity while its geometry shifts to magnetic north. The roof sails above, modulating between the two cartographies while subtly nodding to the southwesterly summer rains.

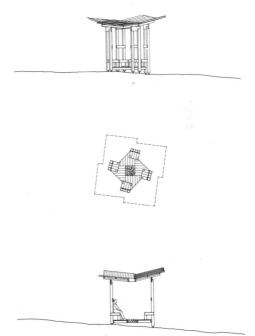

OBSERVATORY
California
1992

Observatory is sited on a hillside ranch overlooking California's Sonoma Valley. Observatory's timber arcade wraps an existing water tank in a twelve-sided polygon that is twenty-four feet in diameter. Atop the arcade, a metal cart runs on steel rails. After climbing the cart's ladder and seating oneself, one wheels about the water tank while framing the heavens with a mask-like sextant.

Observatory is essentially a device for locating oneself within systems both local and galactic. Nestled in the saddle between two prominent hills and wrapping the water tank, the arcade grounds itself to the immediate geography. On a grander scale, the twelve sides of the arcade mark the twelve months of the year. Meanwhile, the elevated cart provides vistas of the surrounding landscape as well as the stars, while its lack of a roof is a continual reminder of the aridity of the climate. At the core of the building, the concrete tank, central to the survival of the ranch during droughts and fires, now also operates as the center of an astronomical chart—its conical roof is inscribed with important site lines. Circumnavigating on a starlit evening, one literally becomes a gauge of time and space, on the earth and in the heavens.

The Observatory has yet to be built. It is intended to dematerialize as it spirals out and up: from the irregular site-cast concrete mass of the reservoir, to the planed Douglas-fir timbers of the arcade, to the light reflective aluminum cladding of the viewing cart.

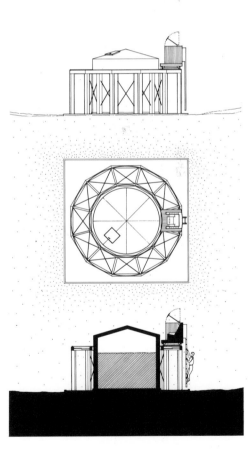

AFTERWORD
Turner Brooks

I have always liked small structures that make large gestures to engage the larger landscape. Mike Cadwell's structures do exactly that.

The small buildings by Cadwell are stripped and elemental. They are condensed into a kind of essence of building where the power of the act of building, and the ceremonial aspect of the thing that is made, come together in such a way that each is celebrated by the other. While they are about the process of construction, each of these little buildings also involves a special choreographed ritual that relates it to a particular place in the larger world. Or even, sometimes, beyond this world: House-Tunnel slips out of the ground to align its one window exactly with the winter solstice sun as it sets behind a distant ridge.

These structures, all made from raw, rough-cut, "green" lumber, speak emphatically about how to make something in a clearly expressed and logical way. They tell about wood joining wood, joints notched or bolted or simply nailed, with a frankness that could be described as crude and elegant all at once. The chunky members of the truss of the Bridge-Box, for example, tumble gracefully up and over the small stream below, their big shiny bolt heads gleaming through the panel points on the raw wood. There is sometimes an irrational element in the shear bulk of the individual members. The muscular little Rolling Tower lurks in its rubble surrounds like some stunted medieval war machine. This "clumsy" exaggeration is also seen in the furniture pieces, especially the chairs, where elephantine legs are held off the ground by little swiveling wheels that give a light exuberance to their mass. Chained together they dance and swivel about on their tiny feet. There is, in fact, a kind of clumsy grace to much of Cadwell's work.

Cadwell's little buildings satisfy a fundamental instinct for inhabitation that goes back to one's childhood. They are the descendants of rude tiny dwellings made out of pillows, blankets, and overturned furniture constructed in the larger adult landscape of a living room. They are also descended from childhood tree houses (Cadwell made a famous one at his ancestral home in Pittsford, Vermont). Whether through a screen of leaves or through cracks between pillows, the world "out there" always seems more accessible when cozily ensconced inside. With Cadwell's structures there is a place for the body, snugly contained, and a resulting sense of empowerment over the domain viewed outside. Part of the sense of peaceful containment in the interiors of both Cadwell's work and its precedents results from it being finally reached after a slightly acrobatic act of getting there.

I have a particularly close relationship to Drum-Barge, as it was launched and floated in the pond not far from my house. One day late in the summer, Mike arrived at the dam at the end of the pond with a Toyota pick-up truck full of wooden pieces—the kit of parts for Drum-Barge. With one assistant the structure was assembled within a matter of hours, pieces fitting together like some huge-scale Japanese wood puzzle. The next day Mike's entire entourage of hefty brothers arrived to assist with a ceremonial launching. Drum-Barge floated and, blown by the wind, staked out its watery domain. The canvas roof, catching the shifting gusts of wind, glided this way and that against the horizon of distant hills. The structure was entered from underneath by swimming between the pontoons, grasping a rope suspended from the pyramidal roof, then pulling oneself up through a diaphanous cone-shaped orifice (the canted plywood walls of this magical zone dappled and dissolved in the reflections from the rippling water below), and arriving on the floor of the interior located some three feet above the water level. Crouching, one could gaze out of the four small portals cut into the boards surrounding the barrel; standing, one could lean one's arms over the top of the barrel and, shaded by the canvas roof, be wafted gently by the winds around the pond.

On one occasion my entire family of five was entertained to a very elegant dinner in the surprisingly roomy interior of the drum. On a warm summer day the heads of four men were seen symmetrically disposed around the rim of the drum while four delicate jets trickled out of the four small windows. In late November, on a freezing blustery day, a visiting family of eight, dressed in extravagantly furry overcoats and wool hats, cast off and made a speedy crossing over frothy whitecaps just before the pond froze over. Then the structure froze into the ice, tilted slightly, and became the occasional warming hut for skaters on the pond. The flanks of the pontoons reflected the sun and in the spring the first open water appeared around them. Soon Drum-Barge floated free again, bobbing in its own small pool of open water. That summer it was anchored by some kids, who paddled under it in their tiny punts as if docking at a huge oil rig. They pulled themselves up into it by the rope, scaled the interior framing of the drum, stood briefly teetering on the rim, and then leaped back into the water, managing always to just avoid crashing into the pontoons.

Grounded now at the shallow end of the pond among cattails, its sides weathered dark, planks beginning to warp, its pontoons awash and the bright canvas roof long since blown away, Drum-Barge stands listing to one side, still presiding over its old domain.

Pamphlet Architecture was initiated in 1977 as an independent vehicle to criticize, question, and exchange views. Each issue is assembled by an individual author/architect. For more information, pamphlet proposals, or contributions please write to Pamphlet Architecture, 435 Hudson Street, 4th fl., NY, NY 10014.

Pamphlet Architecture is distributed exclusively by Princeton Architectural Press, 37 East 7th Street, NY, NY 10003. Telephone (212) 995-9620.

PAMPHLETS PUBLISHED:

★*out of print*